CW00422325

WALTHAMSTOW AND LEYTON TRAMWAYS

Robert J Harley

MP Middleton Press

Cover Picture: Two trams pause outside the Bakers Arms in this picture taken on 24th August 1938, when the tramways of Leyton were enjoying an Indian summer before succumbing totally to the trolleybus. (H.B.Priestley)

Cover Colours: These reflect the dark green and primrose livery applied to cars of the Leyton Council Tramways fleet.

First published November 1995

ISBN 1 873793 65 0

© Middleton Press 1995

Design - Deborah Goodridge

Published by Middleton Press
   Easebourne Lane
   Midhurst
   West Sussex
   GU29 9AZ
   Tel: 01730 813169
   Fax: 01730 812601

Printed & bound by Biddles Ltd,
   Guildford and Kings Lynn

CONTENTS

Leyton Tramways   1- 50
Walthamstow Tramways   51-120

PART 1 - LEYTON TRAMWAYS

Thatched House to Bakers Arms   1
Lea Bridge Road   15
Whipps Cross   26
Leytonstone   38
Power Supply   42
Rolling Stock   43

PART 2 - WALTHAMSTOW TRAMWAYS

Rising Sun to Napier Arms   51
The Bell, Walthamstow   59
Hoe Street   64
Royal Standard to Higham Hill   73
St.James's Street to Markhouse Road 78
Ferry Boat Inn   84
Walthamstow Depot to
                    Chingford Mount 88
Rolling Stock   102
Finale   118

INTRODUCTION AND ACKNOWLEDGEMENTS

My gratitude goes to all the photographers mentioned in the credits, their work has preserved a way of life now long gone. I would particularly like to thank Terry Russell for his help in preparing car drawings. Local experts Rod Roke and C.D.Mason have added to the total of my knowledge and tramway stalwart D.W.K.Jones has patiently answered all my enquiries. Pictures have been supplied from the extensive collections of B.J.Cross, Dave Jones and J.H.Price. Once again I am indebted to Rosy Thacker of the National Tramway Museum for supplying material from the NTM's extensive archive and to G.Croughton for supplying tickets. Pictures from the collection of the late Alan Watkins have been kindly lent by Ann Watkins.

GEOGRAPHICAL SETTING

The River Lea, which flows into the Thames at Poplar, forms the boundary on the western side of Walthamstow and Leyton. The ancient Epping Forest is prominent on the eastern flanks of the area. Both local authorities were once administered by the county of Essex, but since 1965 they have formed the London Borough of Waltham Forest.

Detailed street maps are to the scale 1:2500 unless otherwise stated.

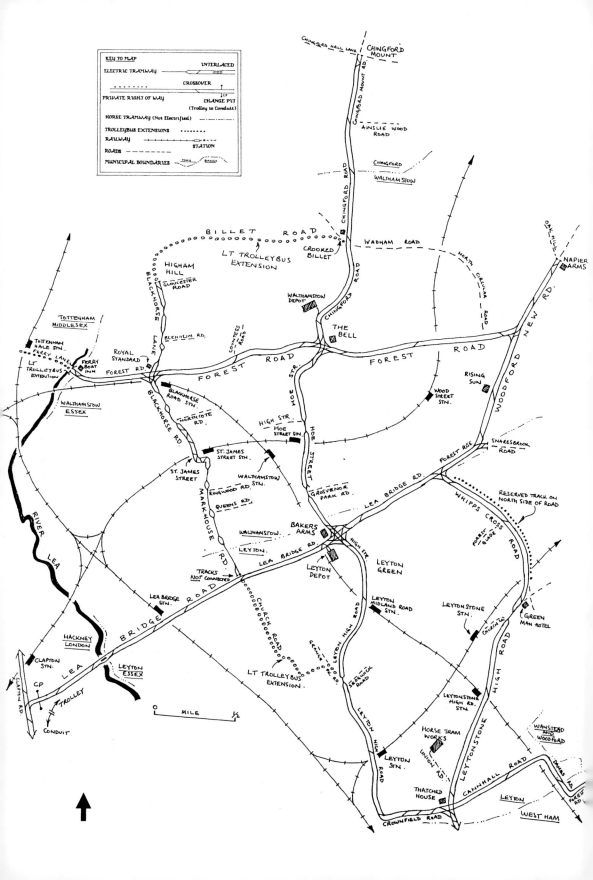

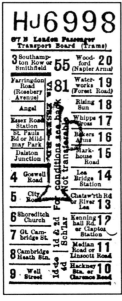

Map of tram services and route details as
published by London Transport in 1935.

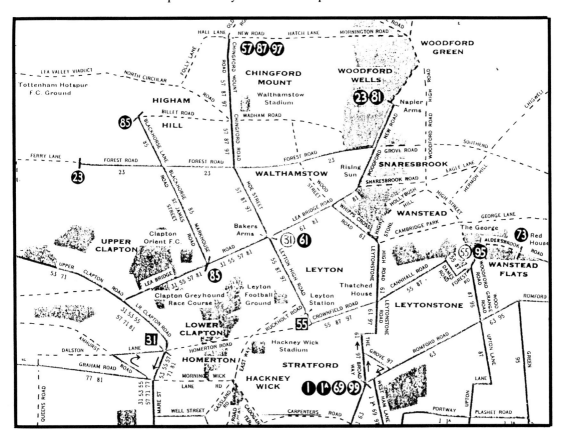

HISTORICAL BACKGROUND

Horse cars operated by the North Metropolitan Tramways Company, first arrived in Leytonstone from Stratford in January 1872. This event coincided with the construction of a repair and tramcar building works in Union Road which opened in 1876.

Finally the North Met horse line reached the Green Man, Leytonstone in August 1881. On the other side of town in May 1883 a service began along Lea Bridge Road and by 1892 horse trams belonging to the Lea Bridge, Leyton and Walthamstow Tramways Company were traversing tracks from the Rising Sun Inn to Upper Clapton, and from Bakers Arms to Leyton Station. However, horse traction had its limitations and the twentieth century ushered in the electric era which promised much for the new urban districts and municipalities. Construction work for new electric lines commenced in 1904. The citizens of Walthamstow were provided with a five minute service on the following routes inaugurated on 3rd June 1905:

Chingford to Bakers Arms

Ferry Lane to Napier Arms, Woodford

Markhouse Road to Higham Hill

Rising Sun to Napier Arms (commenced operation shortly after the other three services)

In Leyton electric services started on 1st December 1906 with the opening of the sections:

Clapton, Lea Bridge to the Rising Sun

Bakers Arms to Wanstead Flats

Clapton, Lea Bridge to Bow Bridge via Whipps Cross

Leytonstone, Green Man to Bow Bridge

The last two services were operated jointly with West Ham Corporation. Horse trams were still worked from Lea Bridge to Cornthwaite Road, Clapton.

It will be noted that although both councils ran trams to the Rising Sun Inn, there was no track connection at this point. The Walthamstow shuttle service from Waterworks Corner/ Forest Road to the Rising Sun was poorly patronised, and the situation was further aggravated by the fact that Leyton services to the Rising Sun ran spasmodically, sometimes only on Sunday for trippers to Epping Forest. Needless to say, the competing bus services had a field day over this section!

In the years preceding the First World War, connections with lines owned by the LCC and West Ham allowed through services to be worked into Central London and to the Victoria and Albert Docks. In January 1913 the following network was operated:

- *Chingford to Stratford*
7 *Bakers Arms to V&A Docks via Stratford*
8 *Bakers Arms to V&A Docks via Forest Gate*
55 *Bloomsbury to Bakers Arms via Hackney*
57 *Moorgate to Bakers Arms via Hackney*
61 *Aldgate to Bakers Arms via Leytonstone*

The stresses and strains of providing public transport during the First World War took their toll on both councils and in the 1920s the situation looked grim. Leyton opted for an agreement with the LCC whereby the larger operator undertook to restore and supply rolling stock. This arrangement commenced in July 1921. Walthamstow on the other hand decided to remain in control of its own system and a comprehensive reconstruction plan involving track doubling and new rolling stock was pursued. Further signs of a tramway renaissance in East London showed in the commitment to improved joint services and the long overdue connection of Walthamstow and Leyton tracks at the Rising Sun. However, this seemingly rosy future was interrupted by the formation of London Transport in 1933.

The new owners of the local tramways soon made it clear that these would be replaced by trolleybuses. This process started with the abandonment of the Woodford to Ferry Lane service in October 1936. As the programme progressed, an area was put aside for tram scrapping at Walthamstow Depot. The local tramtracks finally fell silent with the conversion of service 61 on 5th November 1939. The more modern eight wheel cars from the former Walthamstow and Leyton fleets were transferred to other duties and most survived until the final months of the South London lines in 1951/52.

1. Leyton Tramways

THATCHED HOUSE TO BAKERS ARMS

1.   What better way to start our journey than with a celebration! This splendid procession marks the inauguration of the Leyton system on 1st December 1906. Leyton had the foresight to order top covered cars which were more attractive to passengers in inclement weather. Out of the 40 trams on order, 28 were available for the opening and brisk trade was experienced after the ceremonies were over. (A.J.Watkins Coll.)

2. LCC car 922 heads south on service 61; on the left a Leyton vehicle waits in Crownfield Road to cross the junction at Thatched House. This location is also featured in picture 79 of companion Middleton Press album *East Ham and West Ham Tramways*. (B.J.Cross Coll.)

3.   On 22nd December 1906, new Leyton tracks in Dames Road and Forest Road were joined to the West Ham metals in Woodford Road which are pictured in the foreground of this view. Leyton car 52 has been renovated by the LCC in the early 1920s and it bears the gold letters LCC on the waist panel. Other sister vehicles retained the Leyton Council monogram which was deemed more sensitive to the feelings of local populus who resented the take over by "big brother" in the shape of the London County Council.
(G.N.Southerden)

4. The London Transport regime is in place in this mid-1930s scene of car 1436 perched on the railway bridge at Leyton Station. This tram began its career in 1910 on the Eltham service of the LCC, and is pictured in its original maroon lake and primrose livery in the Tramway Classics volume, *Greenwich and Dartford Tramways.* (C.Carter)

G.E.R Station, Le

5. The driver of Leyton car 41 turns to check all is well before he moves away from the stop by Leyton Station. On the approach to the bridge, a West Ham vehicle descends after having passed another Leyton car.
(B.J.Cross Coll.)

6. In the days when the tramcar was "king of the road", we observe West Ham car 98 as it makes its way past the Methodist Church on the corner with High Road, Leyton. Covering the tram's headlight is a number which indicates that this car is on service 7.
(B.J.Cross Coll.)

7. The Bakers Arms junction is pictured here with track laying at an advanced stage...one hopes the foreman notices that one of the point blades is missing before the road surface is reinstated! (D.Jones Coll.)

8. Horses wait patiently for passengers to board before they begin the leisurely trot along Lea Bridge Road to the terminus at Clapton. This rather sedate form of transport was already outmoded by the time that this scene was recorded in 1905. (R.J.Harley Coll.)

9.   Mechanical road vehicles have already made an impact on the travelling public as car 70 looms up behind the competing motor bus registered AN 536. Although the tram was likely to be more reliable, the bus had the advantage of offering a through service to Oxford Circus, a facility which the electric vehicle could not match. (B.J.Cross Coll.)

10. Three large LCC bogie cars dominate the Bakers Arms intersection with a somewhat smaller B type bus on route 38 to Victoria in attendance. Tram service 81 started in early 1915 and connected Bloomsbury with the Bakers Arms; on Sundays it was extended to the Rising Sun primarily for excursionists to the Epping Forest. (R.J.Harley Coll.)

11. The Hoe Street to High Street, Leyton tracks were converted to trolleybuses in June 1937 just over a year before this view was taken of car 1205 waiting for the green light to proceed along Lea Bridge Road in the direction of the Napier Arms, Woodford. (H.B.Priestley)

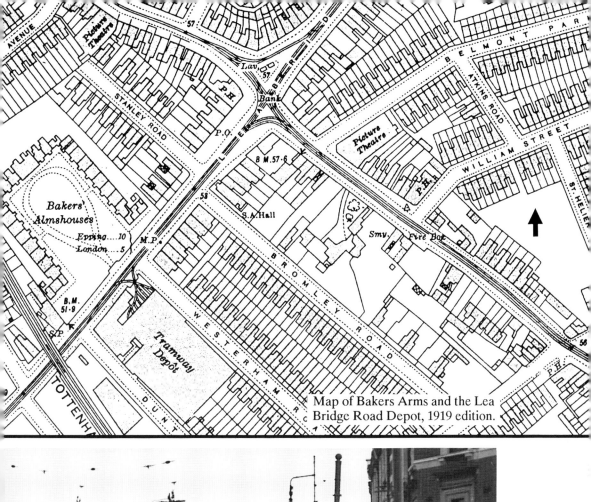

Map of Bakers Arms and the Lea
Bridge Road Depot, 1919 edition.

12. Looking west towards the depot we are treated to the spectacle of car 907 on service 81, followed by an E3 class car on service 31. The former service gave way to trolleybuses on 11th June 1939, whilst the Kingsway Subway service 31 was cut back to Hackney on the same date. (H.B.Priestley)

13. The photographer has now moved to the north east side of the junction where car 198 occupies the terminal siding of service 61. The beautiful condition of this car, supplied new to Leyton in 1931, will be noted. It met a fiery end at Penhall Road, Charlton in the summer of 1952. (H.B.Priestley)

1054.—TRANSFER AT BAKERS ARMS.

HACKNEY, LEYTON, WALTHAMSTOW AND WEST HAM DEPOTS.

A complaint has been made that a passenger holding a 5d. workman return ticket issued for a journey between Plaistow Broadway and High Street, Walthamstow, was refused a transfer at " Bakers Arms " on the return journey when boarding a Service No. 97 car at High Street, Walthamstow, on the grounds that this car was proceeding to his destination.

This passenger desired to travel to Stopford Road on Service No. 87, and all concerned are instructed that the transfer must be permitted in similar cases.

LT circular from May 1936

14. The tram furthest from the camera is working service 57 after it had been curtailed because the section from Bakers Arms to Chingford had been converted to trolleybuses. The conductor of the service 61 car puts up one trolley whilst the motorman ties down the leading one. The equiping of many London trams with one trolley for each direction did away with the performance of swinging the pole at termini. (H.B.Priestley)

LEA BRIDGE ROAD

→

16. The frantic activity to get the depot ready in time seems to have come to a temporary halt whilst this scene is preserved for posterity. In the centre of the picture are placed the stanchions to support the rails either side of the maintenance pits. (D.Jones Coll.)

15. On the right is Leyton Depot with the Bakers Arms junction in the background. LCC car 1191 is passing the car shed entrance. (B.J.Cross Coll.)

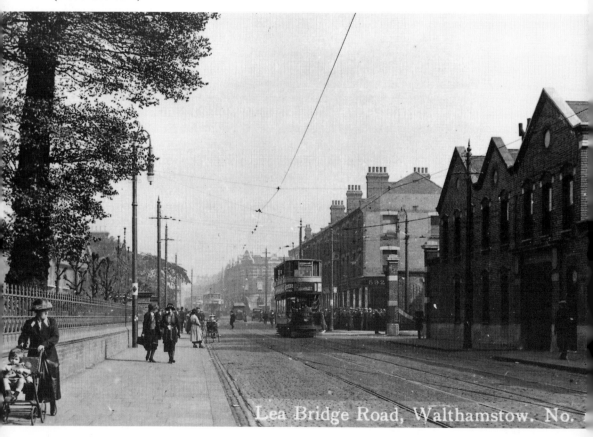

Lea Bridge Road, Walthamstow. No.

Original construction plan of Leyton Depot

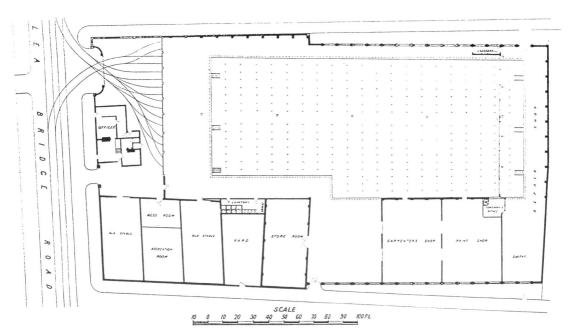

Plan of Car Shed.

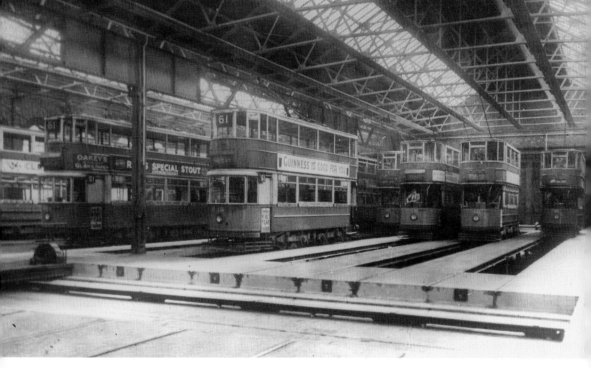

17. From 1906 to December 1908 the horse cars on the right of this depot interior were kept to maintain the remnants of the Lea Bridge to Clapton service before electrification. This is an age when the depot foreman kept the place spick and span. Woe betide any fitter who left his tools out of their racks or who deposited axle box grease on the floor! (D.Jones Coll.)

18. Alterations to the depot were started in 1930. The LCC intended to use the new E3 bogie cars and these required the installation of a traverser which was regarded as standard equipment in any LCC car shed. The depot was also home to a number of M class four wheel cars; in later London Transport days cars from here worked services 55, 57, 61 and 81. (W.A.Camwell)

19. We take a final look before the contractors occupy the site to convert the building to trolleybus operation. This involved some expensive work on the foundations with the repositioning of the roof pillars; the last tram vacated the site on 11th June 1939. The life span of the replacement vehicles was barely 20 years and their tenure ended in April 1959 when routes 555 and 581 disappeared in favour of diesel buses. (W.A.Camwell)

20. The bridge over the River Lea once marked the boundary between the Counties of London and Essex. Here an LT car on service 55 gains the London side. Note the split carriageway over the bridge. (C.Carter)

21. We witness a turn of the century scene at the horse tramway terminus opposite Cornthwaite Road, Clapton, as a car of the Lea Bridge, Leyton and Walthamstow Tramwys Co. prepares to depart. This was a most inconveniently situated terminal and on electrification the rails were extended to form a junction with the LCC conduit lines in Lower Clapton Road.
(B.J.Cross Coll.)

22. At the western end of Lea Bridge Road a change pit existed where trams changed current collection from the overhead to conduit methods. The car on the right is about to turn southwards for Central London on a joint service which came into being on 1st July 1910. The through tracks in the centre of this view carry LCC cars from Hackney to Stamford Hill. (D.Jones Coll.)

23. We now retrace our steps to arrive with car 1635 at the crossover by Copeland Road, to the east of Bakers Arms. Wires for both trolleybuses and trams have been erected and traction standards have been painted with a double white band. Older poles lacking these marks will be removed by LT workmen in the next few days. Between the tram and the commercial tricycle is a fire alarm pillar. (C.Carter)

24. Just a few yards futher on from the previous photo, we see a smartly turned out motorman standing next to car 1964. Shortly he will reboard his car, then apply power to negotiate the crossover at the start of the return journey to Battersea in South West London. Passengers on this run would be transported through the Kingsway Subway and out on to the Embankment before crossing the Thames at Westminster Bridge. (D.W.K.Jones)

25. Another reversal on Lea Bridge Road is car 650 which has its own death notice on the rocker panel at the far end of the car. This will inform the travelling public of the imminent conversion of service 55 to trolleybuses. (A.B.Cross)

WHIPPS CROSS

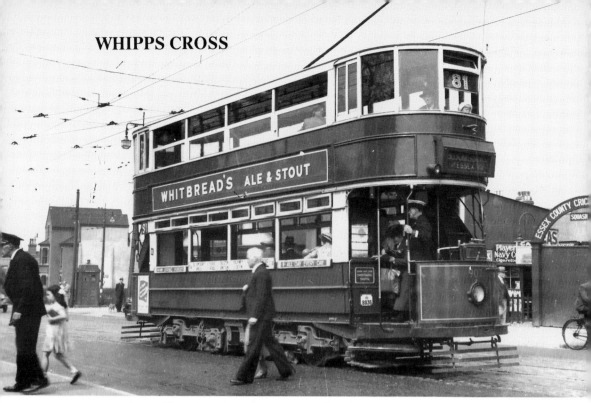

26. Car 907 is positioned at the triangular junction with Whipps Cross Road. Note the conductor helping passengers disembark. In this July 1938 scene there was very little traffic to disturb the summer's day. (H.B.Priestley)

27. LCC car 1327 crosses from Forest Rise into Lea Bridge Road. The destination of the car is Moorgate and the fare from Whipps Cross to the City is a princely thrupence ha'penny (just over 1p!). Regular LCC working began on this section in 1910, but journeys past Bakers Arms to the Rising Sun were later restricted to Saturday afternoons and Sundays only. (A.P.Wire)

28. We look north from Whipps Cross Road, in this first of three views taken at the same location. Here tracklaying is in progress. This construction work was completed by gangs of labourers and permanent way men who had practically no mechanical assistance. Tasks were carried out manually, the preparation of the track bed had to be inch perfect and the gauge of the rails spot on...a standard four feet eight and a half inches. (W.E.Wright)

29. The original tracks along Whipps Cross Road were positioned in the carriageway as shown here. During the early 1920s improvements to the layout resulted in reserved double track on the north side of the public road. (J.H.Price Coll.)

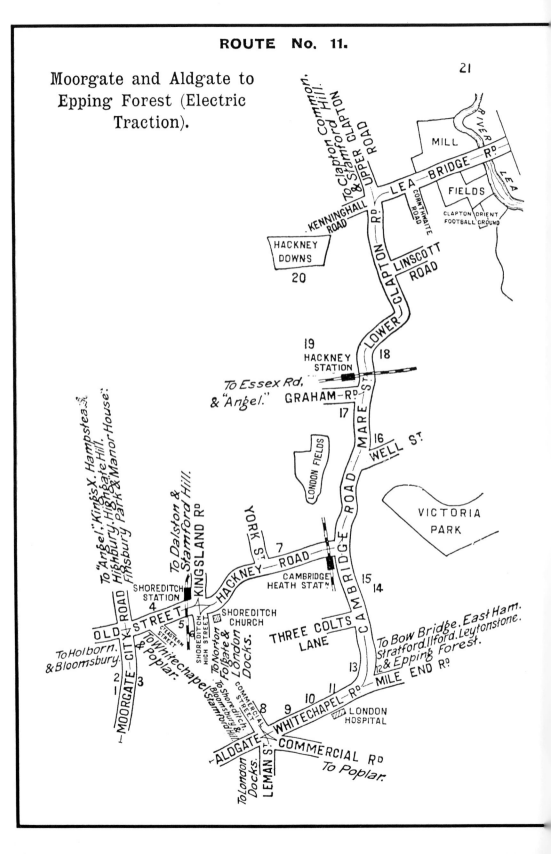

ROUTE No. 11.

Moorgate and Aldgate to Epping Forest (Electric Traction).

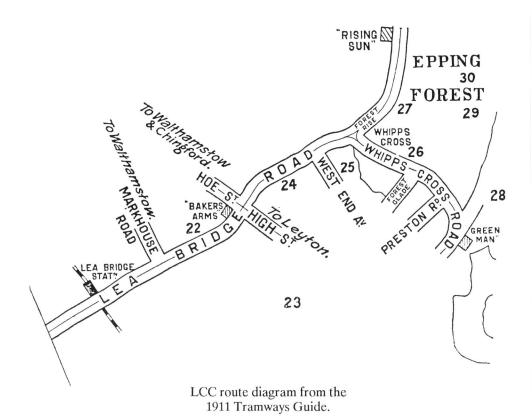

LCC route diagram from the
1911 Tramways Guide.

1. Honourable Artillery Company.
2. Bunhill Fields.
3. Wesley's Chapel.
4. Shoreditch Technical Institute.
5. Shoreditch Town Hall.
6. Shoreditch Olympia.
7. North-Eastern Hospital.
8. Toynbee Hall.
9. Whitechapel Art Gallery.
10. Stepney Borough Museum.
11. Pavilion Theatre.
12. Trinity Almshouses.
13. Foresters' Music Hall.
14. Bethnal Green Gardens.
15. Bethnal Green Museum.
16. Lady Holles' School.
17. Hackney Empire.
18. Hackney Old Church.
19. Hackney Institute.
20. Hackney Downs Secondary School.
21. East London Water Works.
22. Almshouses.
23. Essex County Cricket Ground.
24. Knotts Green.
25. West Ham Union Infirmary.
26. Hollow Pond.
27. Forest School.
28. Weavers' Almshouses.
29. Infant Orphan Asylum.
30. Eagle Pond.

30. This final shot shows two ex-Leyton E3 class cars now repainted in London Transport red and cream livery. The weather has obviously turned out warmer than expected as a coat hangs on the opposite traction standard. Passengers on board this Aldgate bound 61 can expect a fast run along the reserved track to Leytonstone. (D.W.K.Jones)

31. A short detour brings us to Forest Rise in 1905 as the new rails stretch out on the extension to Woodford New Road and the Rising Sun Inn. (W.E.Wright)

32. The Rising Sun marked the end of Leyton tracks and on Sundays trams would bring many folk from less salubrious surroundings to enjoy the delights and cleaner air of Epping Forest. Unfortunately a further trip along this road demanded a change of car as the Walthamstow metals were unconnected with those of Leyton Council. (D.Jones Coll.)

33. Brisk traffic is expected and cars are being loaded as they arrive at the stop. Trams were unsurpassed in their ability to move masses of people with the minimum of fuss. Above car 206, a section feed supplies power to the overhead wires. (H.B.Priestley)

34. As the trolleybus replacement scheme took hold so new traffic arrangements like this roundabout at Whipps Cross became necessary for providing turning circles for the new vehicles. Service 61 remains untouched by this activity although its days are numbered and soon trolleybus tandards will be erected along Whipps Cross Road and the tramway reserved track will be abandoned. (C.Carter)

35. On a spring day in 1938, the trees by Hollow Pond are about to burst into leaf. This scene gives the lie to the notion that tramrides in the metropolis were totally urban in character. Here the April sunshine catches car 189 as it slows for the photographer in a setting so different from the streets of the East End where it began its journey. (W.A.Camwell)

36. A Summer Sunday in Whipps Cross Road and the trams are doing good business serving the needs of hikers and families out for a pleasure ride. In an era of restricted motor car ownership, a trip on service 61 provided a cheap afternoon outing. The wiring on this section was carried on single bracket arms to minimise wayleave payments demanded by the Conservators of Epping Forest for each traction standard. (D.A.Thompson)

LEYTONSTONE

37. We now reach the southern end of Whipps Cross Road in Leytonstone. Car 34 advertises a rather circuitous service from the River Lea, Clapton to Bow Bridge calling at Epping Forest, Leytonstone and Stratford en route. (D.Jones Coll.)

38. A late 1920s view of a Leyton green car appropriately posed at the Green Man, Leytonstone. Note the LCC type side destination board for service 61 and the Leyton Council monogram in the centre of the car's waist panel. The plough carrier is attached on the right hand side of the four wheel truck. (H.A.Whitcombe)

39. Time has moved on since the last picture and car 210 is seen in July 1938 in Leytonstone High Road. (H.B.Priestley)

40. A few moments after the previous photograph and we observe car 190 Citybound for Aldgate. Note the wonderful array of period fashions and motor vehicles; on the extreme left of shot is an advisory message for motorists. (H.B.Priestley)

41. We finish our exploration of Leyton Council Tramways with this picture of Leytonstone High Road in 1907. The open top tram is a West Ham vehicle on a joint working to Bow Bridge. LCC electric tracks became available on 11th May 1910 for the through service to Aldgate. (A.Anderson)

POWER SUPPLY

Underground feeder cables acted as an electrical distribution network. The diagram shown here first appeared in an article in the *Tramway and Railway World* journal for 6th December 1906. It details how current was supplied to the tramway system from a central power station, where generating equipment was situated. (Companion Middleton Press albums *Southend-on-Sea Tramways* and *Dover's Tramways* contain pictures of generating sets.) Cables from the power station to the tram route were usually laid in pipes, sometimes of the Doulton fire clay variety, underneath pavements. The supply to the overhead was effected through a section box (see pictures 52 and 88) situated by the side of the road. Power was then conveyed via an insulated wire attached to the nearest traction standard and from there to the running wires and trolleyhead of the tramcar. Interestingly much of this network survived to be used by the replacing trolleybuses and indeed the existence of these distribution circuits probably had some influence in the extension of trolleybus wires over previous tramless areas such as Church Road. In many parts of London these "ready made" ex-tramway feeder channels have taken on new life as the recipients of miles of fibre optic cable for the TV and information technology age.

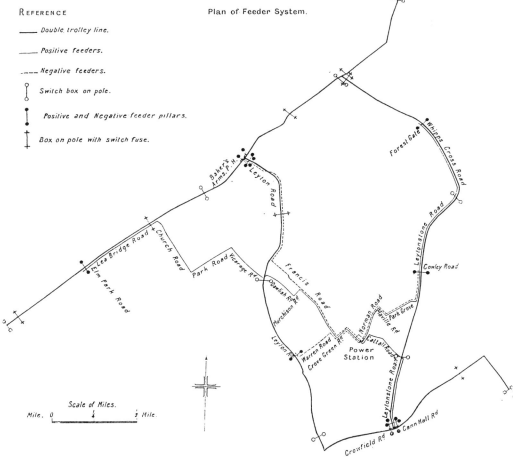

REFERENCE   Plan of Feeder System.

——— *Double trolley line.*

——— *Positive feeders.*

- - - *Negative feeders.*

Switch box on pole.

Positive and Negative feeder pillars.

Box on pole with switch fuse.

Scale of Miles.

Mile. 0   ¼   ½ Mile.

The **feeder system** includes all the cables necessary to distribute the current from the generating station or substation to the working conductors; in the overhead system it consists of the trolley wires and the track rails. In compliance with the Board of Trade regulations, the trolley wire is divided into ½-mile sections insulated from one another, and the connection with the feeder system is usually made at the centre or ends of each section.

In the conduit system, which has an insulated return, the negative feeders are duplicates of the positive feeders; but in the overhead system, which has an earthed return, the negative feeder system differs from the positive, and requires separate consideration. In Great Britain, feeder cables are laid underground, but in America, on the Continent, and in the Colonies they are run overhead. They usually follow the line of track, but considerable saving may sometimes be effected by taking a short cut between the power station and the feeding point ; this means not only a saving in the cost of the feeder, but also in the watts lost in transmission. Any of the standard types of underground mains may be used for feeders.

Feeder Pillars.—The positive feeder terminates on a small switchboard placed in a cast-iron box, called a **feeder, or switch, pillar**, which is placed on the footpath near the point at which connection is to be made to the trolley wire. The short feeders connecting the main feeder with the trolley wire are called **line taps, or side feed-cables**. They are usually drawn inside one of the poles used for supporting the trolley wire ; and from the pole they pass along either the bracket arm or span wire to a feeder ear attached to the overhead wire. These line taps are connected to a feeder bus-bar in the switch pillar through trolley switches, which are used when necessary for cutting the current off the overhead wire.

42. The power feed arrangements for both "up" and "down" tracks can be clearly seen to the right of the tram. This is the stop on Whipps Cross Road opposite Forest Glade. (D.Jones Coll.)

ROLLING STOCK

A more detailed account of the Leyton and Walthamstow fleets is contained in "The Tramways of East London" by "Rodinglea", published in 1967. Readers are directed to this work and to a series of articles by the late V.E.Burrows in the *Tramway Review* for 1953/54 for added information on car types.

Cars 1-10. These were horse cars retained to operate the Clapton service until electrification. They were built at Preston in 1899 and had transverse "garden" seats on the top deck; the livery was red and cream.

Cars 11-70. These were covered top, four wheel cars built by Milnes, Voss and Co.; they were equipped with Mountain and Gibson radial trucks of 8ft. 6ins./2590mm wheelbase. Seating was for 22 in the lower saloon and for 26 in the enclosed upper saloon, with spaces for five persons on each balcony. The first batch of cars (11-50) were delivered in 1906 to be followed by cars 51-70 in 1907. Cars 31-70 were later modified to include a plough carrier to work over the LCC conduit lines. Withdrawal of these vehicles began with the LCC take over in 1921 and by 1931 they had disappeared from service.

Cars 161-210. Delivered during 1931, these trams belonged to the E3 class then being introduced to the streets of London by the LCC. They were all enclosed, eight wheel vehicles with seats for 74 passengers. As trolleybus substitution progressed, so these cars were transferred south of the river and most lasted until the final day of London's trams, 5th July 1952.

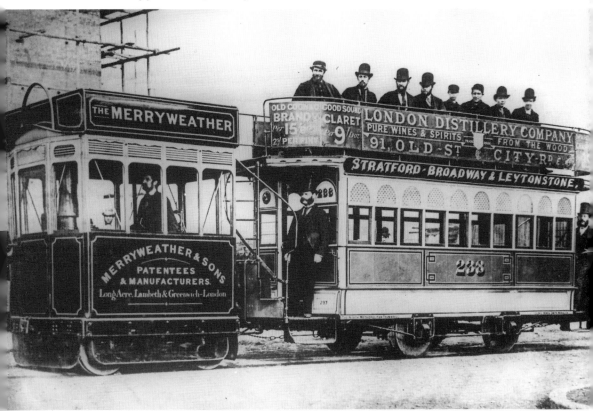

43. An early experiment in mechanical traction is pictured here in 1877. This Merryweather steam tramway loco took the place of the horses as it attempted to pull car 238 from Stratford to Leytonstone and back. The trials, which were inconclusive, were watched by a Parliamentary Select Committee gathering evidence for legislation governing the application of mechanical power to tramways. (National Tramway Museum)

44. This horse car was one of the ten retained for the Clapton service. Note the gold letters on the waist panel denoting ownership by Leyton Urban District Council. Seating inside was on facing benches and outside on the top deck travellers were accommodated on transverse seats. (A.J.Watkins Coll.)

45. Car 27 is shown in its original condition, sporting the Leyton dark green and primrose livery. The truck was also painted green. Curtains were provided for the convenience of lower saloon passengers, whilst the upper saloon, where all the smokers congregated, had the benefits of generous "air conditioning", as can be observed in this photo! (Leyton official photo)

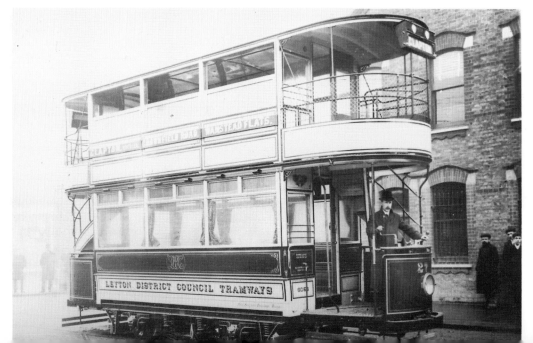

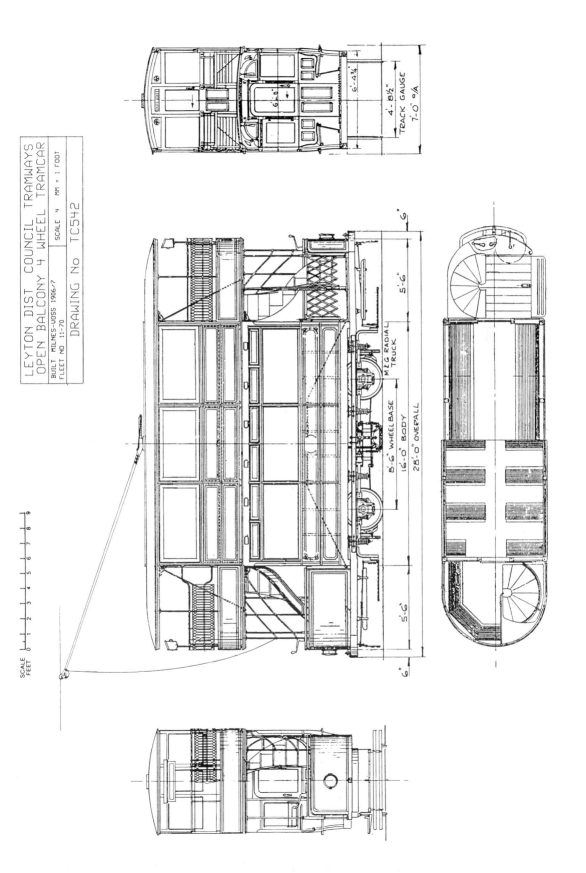

LEYTON DIST COUNCIL TRAMWAYS
OPEN BALCONY 4 WHEEL TRAMCAR

BUILT MILNES-VOSS 1906/7 | SCALE 4 | MM = 1 FOOT

FLEET NO 11-70

DRAWING No TC542

SCALE
FEET 0 1 2 3 4 5 6 7 8 9

6'-4¾"

4'-8½"

TRACK GAUGE

7'-0" P/A

6'-8"

6"

5'-6"

M&G RADIAL TRUCK

8'-6" WHEELBASE

16'-0" BODY

28'-0" OVERALL

5'-6"

6"

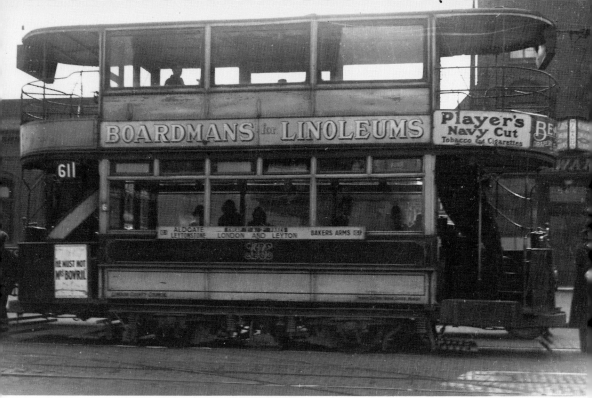

46. The legal lettering at the foot of the rocker panel indicates that ownership is now vested with the LCC. This car is in final condition and is seen here working over conduit track in Mile End Road.   (C.F.Klapper)

47. There is evidence that car 37 has been renovated by the LCC; metal straps and brackets have been fitted to brace the upper and lower decks. This picture was taken around 1928/29. (H.A.Whitcombe)

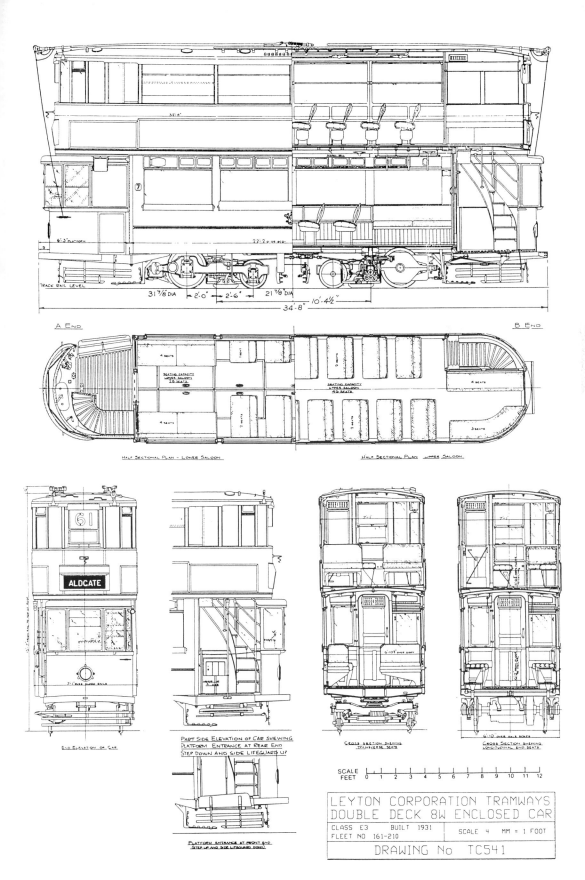

LEYTON CORPORATION TRAMWAYS
DOUBLE DECK 8W ENCLOSED CAR

CLASS E3	BUILT 1931	SCALE 4 MM = 1 FOOT
FLEET No 161-210		

DRAWING No TC541

48. After acquisition by London Transport, ex-Leyton E3 car 192 was painted in an experimental colour scheme of blue and cream, the former colour being described as a shade between light and medium. The LT motif on the side was in the form of a gold lightning flash. This attractive combination was not adopted by LT for the rest of the fleet, although blue was used for some interior repaints. (D.W.K.Jones)

49. Leyton E3 car 186 in LT red and cream livery is depicted with its original windscreens, side service number indicator boxes, unmasked headlights and upper deck advert mouldings. (D.W.K.Jones)

50. Captured on film in March 1952, car 200 is near the end of its life. Note the changes from the pre-war condition, especially the less attractive windscreens and the headlamp masks which LT never removed after the wartime blackout. (J.C.Gillham)

2. Walthamstow Tramways
RISING SUN TO NAPIER ARMS

51. Leyton car 70 and Walthamstow car 27 stand next to one another outside the Rising Sun in Woodford New Road. Although it is not clear from this photograph, the tracks of the two systems were not connected. However, that doesn't seem to matter much in this peaceful Edwardian summer of long ago. (B.J.Cross Coll.)

52. Just south of Waterworks Corner, car 1205 waits at the stop in Woodford New Road. The tram will then edge forward a couple of feet before the motorman shuts off power to coast under the section feed which runs from the tall metal section box on the pavement to the left of the picture. Another electric vehicle in the shape of a 623 trolleybus turns into Forest Road. (H.B.Priestley)

53. An inspector, a motorman and a conductor show off their respective uniforms as car 14 stands on the points leading to Forest Road. Note the adverts on the stair risers and the motorman's step fixed in the "up" position to deter passengers from boarding at the driver's end. The track at this spot was doubled in the mid-1920s. (B.J.Cross Coll.)

54. Car 28 seems to have taken the wrong track at this loop in Woodford New Road, but there is so little traffic to worry about that this hardly matters. The whole scene is framed by the trees of Epping Forest; nowadays this area has been ripped apart by new highway and roundabout construction associated with the A406 Southend Road. (J.H.Price Coll.)

55. The conductor of car 38 lends a helping hand before the tram continues in the direction of Woodford. (H.A.Whitcombe)

56. We arrive at the end of the line opposite the Napier Arms, Woodford. Car 20 tarries awhile before the return trip across town to Ferry Lane. Unfortunately proposals to extend the tracks further to Woodford Green came to nothing. (R.J.Harley Coll.)

57. The petrol pumps on the forecourt next to the Napier Arms are a sign that the motor age has begun to gather momentum. Modernity after a fashion has had an impact on car 4 which has been top covered and has received more comfortable transverse seats in the lower saloon. This vehicle was later repainted by London Transport and it was scrapped in 1936/7. (C.F.Klapper)

58. The end of the tramcar is in sight as car 880 waits for its trolley to be turned for the journey back to London. This view also illustrates some of the problems and expense facing LT planners in the provision of new trolleybus facilities. Tramcars are usually double ended so they can be reversed quite easily. However, the two trolleybuses in the background are obliged to use the new turning circle built on land acquired by London Transport. (H.B.Priestley)

THE BELL, WALTHAMSTOW

59. It is Saturday, 3rd June 1905 and the crowds are out to witness the start of the electric era in Walthamstow. Behind car 6 is the Bell Inn which was situated at an important tramway junction. The single track shown here was doubled in 1912/13. (J.H.Price Coll.)

60. In contrast to the previous photo, we are now right at the end of the tramway era as cars 282 and 569 pass under the new trolleybus overhead. (D.W.K.Jones)

61. Car 43 has just passed into LT ownership in this picture dated 25th August 1933, and the letter K has been added after the fleet number. This denoted a former Walthamstow car; this tram was later renumbered 2058. In the foreground an inspector checks his time card. (M.J.O'Connor)

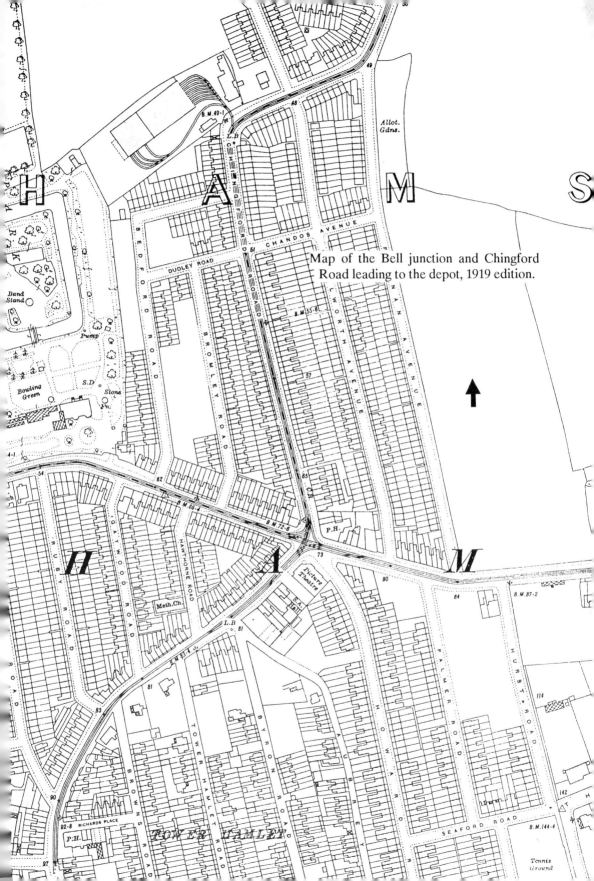

Map of the Bell junction and Chingford Road leading to the depot, 1919 edition.

62. The flags are out at the Bell and they flutter over a scene where the covered top tramcar emerging from Chingford Road constitutes the only traffic of note. (B.J.Cross Coll.)

63. We follow one of the Walthamstow eight wheel cars as it crosses the junction from Hoe Street into Chingford Road. The policeman on point duty has yet to be replaced by traffic lights, but even so he seems to have very little to do. (G.N.Southerden)

HOE STREET

64. Car 8 joins the loop in Hoe Street near to Cairo Road. The Victoria Hall opposite started life as a concert hall in 1897; subsequently it became the venue for watching "animated pictures" as advertised under the TWICE NIGHTLY sign. The Walthamstow area contributed much to the early British film industry and possessed several studios. However, this prowess was short lived and by the 1920s the cameras had moved elsewehere. (J.H.Price Coll.)

HOE ST. WALTHAMSTOW

←————————

65. The first of three views, showing the corner
of Church Hill with Hoe Street, depicts one of
the inaugural cars which toured the system.
(J.H.Price Coll.)

67. Increased traffic, as is borne out by this
photo, has necessitated the extension of the
passing loop in the foreground. However, this
is still a bit of a bottleneck as a southbound car
waits for its opposite number to clear the single
track. From the advertisements on the trams it
would seem that the pre-First World War
building boom is in full swing. ,
(B.J.Cross Coll.)

←————————

66. Public service has now started and this
tramcar is seen in "as delivered" condition.
Note the street sweeper and the horse bus.
(R.J.Harley Coll.)

68. Car 9 pauses by the Tower Hotel on the corner of Selborne Road. This tram achieved some notoriety when it was highjacked by armed gunmen on Saturday, 23rd January 1909. Two desperados forced the conductor to drive the vehicle as they attempted to flee with the booty from a wages snatch. At the end of the day both robbers committed suicide to evade capture; the incident left four people dead and 14 wounded. The stolen payroll which amounted to £80 was never recovered. (R.J.Harley Coll.)

69. In the first weeks of London Transport operation, car 15K crests the railway bridge at Hoe Street Station. This station is now known as Walthamstow Central and the Victoria Underground line was extended to terminate here in 1968. (G.N.Southerden)

70. South of the railway bridge, we encounter
car 5 heading for the Crooked Billet and car 27
with Lea Bridge Road on the indicator blind.
(C.Carter Coll.)

71. This tram has just crossed into Leyton and
is pictured opposite Livingstone Road, a short
distance away from Bakers Arms.
(B.J.Cross Coll.)

72. Walthamstow cars were the first electric trams to reach Bakers Arms. Car 5 is well patronised for the opening of the service in June 1906. The passengers on the Leyton horse car in the distance will have to wait almost another 18 months for their line to be electrified. (D.Jones Coll.)

ROYAL STANDARD TO HIGHAM HILL

73. Crew change time at Royal Standard crossroads where a Woodford bound car waits on the right whilst along Blackhorse Lane a single decker comes into view. (G.N.Southerden)

Map of the Royal Standard area, 1915 edition.

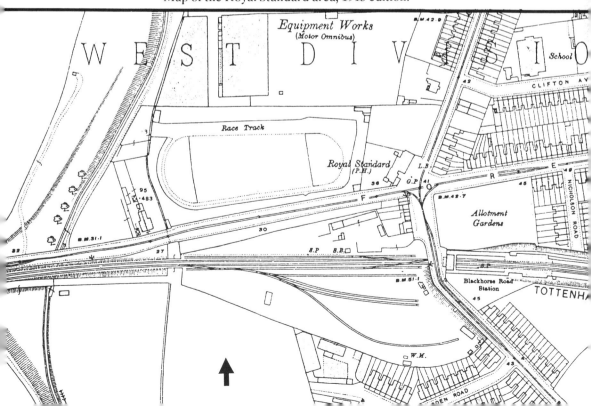

74. The date is 5th July 1929 and car 22 waits on Forest Road for some stragglers to get on, while the conductor is collecting fares on the top deck. This vehicle was one of the last to be treated in the Walthamstow fleet rebuilding programme. It was reconstructed in 1931 and received a new Peckham P35 truck of 8ft. 6ins./2590mm wheelbase. On passing to London Transport it gained the fleet number 2040. (G.N.Southerden)

75. A view taken in October 1936 depicts LT car 2032 about to proceed straight ahead along Forest Road on service 23. New trolleybus standards have been planted outside the shirt factory on the corner of Blackhorse Road. (C.D.Mason)

76. In October 1934, a renumbering scheme resulted in the old Markhouse Road to Higham Hill service 5 becoming LT service 85. This tram turns from Forest Road on its run from the depot to start work. The gradient to the right of the car continues as far as the bridge over the railway at Blackhorse Road Station. (G.N.Southerden)

77. Higham Hill terminus was situated in a quiet suburban road. One of the ex-London United Tramways cars stands with the motorman enjoying the sunshine of this August day in 1929. The arrow below the destination box instructs the crew which side to swing the trolley when reversing. Failure to observe this could result in damage to the main power cable inside the trolley standard on the top deck. (G.N.Southerden)

78. St. James' Street contains a popular shopping area serving the needs of the inhabitants of West Walthamstow. Trams frequently transported locals who, after alighting, then thronged the market stalls which came perilously close to the tramtracks. Another source of short distance passengers was the railway station in the background. (B.J.Cross Coll.)

79. Workmen seem to be busy giving a new lick of paint to the lamp standards and traction poles as car 25 slides past a horse drawn delivery van. (B.J.Cross Coll.)

80. At least single track did leave room for vehicles to park without encroaching on the rails. As motor traffic increased so this type of layout began to tell against the tram, especially when waits at loops slowed the service. (B.J.Cross Coll.)

81. Our vantage point is the front balcony of a tram approaching the terminus in Markhouse Lane. The points are set for the track next to car 2034. (G.N.Southerden)

82. Two trams now occupy the terminal layout, only this time the incoming car has taken the right hand track thus leaving the way clear for car 2041 to depart northwards for Higham Hill. (D.W.K.Jones)

83. The rails in the foreground are laid in Lea Bridge Road and, as can be seen here, are not connected with the tracks in Markhouse Road. This rather pointless situation was remedied by LT when trolleybus route 685 inaugurated a through service across the junction in September 1937. (C.Carter)

LT circular issued in January 1937

1335.—CONVERSION TO TROLLEYBUS—TRAM ROUTE NO. 85— WALTHAMSTOW DEPOT.

Notice to Inspectors and Conductors.

On Sunday, 17th January, 1937, Tram Route No. 85 will be withdrawn and Trolleybus Route No. 685 will be operated between Lea Bridge Road (Markhouse Road) and Walthamstow, "Crooked Billet," via Higham Hill.

FERRY BOAT INN

Fg 1386		
"Bakers' Arms	1d	"Bell" Junction
Hoe str station		Brooks- croft Rd.
"Bell" Junction		Billet Road
Brooks- croft Rd.		Higham Sta Ave
Billet Road		Chingford Mount
Large Rd. Mark house Rd		St... r Street Sta
St James Street Sta		Higham Hill Term

Ticket to be shewn o demand
Available on day of issue only

Walthamstow Council Tramways
Issued subject to the Bye-laws. Available
only on Car on which issued and to
station opposite punch hole

84. Car 1 has arrived outside the Ferry Boat
Inn, whilst a stream of traffic heads in the
opposite direction along Forest Road towards
Walthamstow. (H.A.Whitcombe)

85. Car 2026 stands in front of a sister vehicle at the end of the track facing Ferry Lane. In the background is the bridge over the River Lea which once marked the county boundary between Essex and Middlesex. (J.H.Price Coll.)

86. Car 574 was brought to the area by London Transport; it is one of the 552-601 series trams which are fully described in companion album *Hampstead and Highgate Tramways*. The photo was taken just before service 23 disappeared in favour of trolleybus route 623. (C.Carter)

87. There were many proposals to connect the Walthamstow system with that operating on the Tottenham side of the River Lea. The connection was finally made by other electric vehicles in the shape of the trolleybus. The rails ended outside the Ferry Boat with, latterly, double track containing trailing and facing crossovers. (H.Nicol)

WALTHAMSTOW DEPOT TO CHINGFORD MOUNT

Plan of Walthamstow Depot

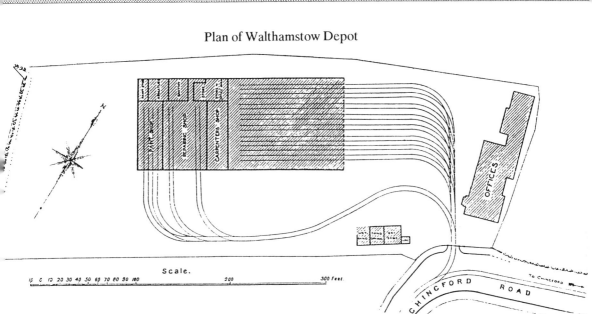

Elevation of offices

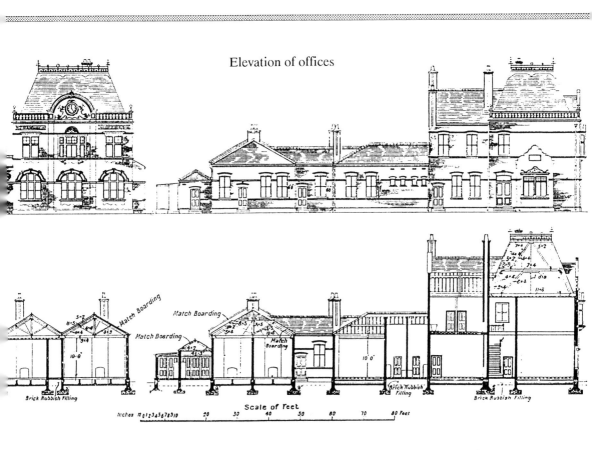

88. A favourite photographic study to enhance municipal pride and to reassure ratepayers of their investment was the depot line up with gleaming, new trams ready for service. Walthamstow Council was no exception when it commissioned this view in 1905, it wanted outsiders to be impressed! The council could also take pride in the lattice girder roof engineered by Peirson and Co., which attracted much favourable publicity in the contemporary technical press, and was cited as "a bold initiative for roofing-in large areas without the necessity for any columns or other internal supports of any kind." (Walthamstow official photo)

89. The gateway on to Chingford Road and the associated tramway office buildings were created with some style. This attention to detail was also manifest in the crests on the section box and ornate base of the adjacent traction standard. (B.J.Cross Coll.)

90. Control of the depot is now in the hands of London Transport as we observe a variety of rolling stock on the track fan leading to the car sheds. Nearest the camera is works car 014, which was constructed in 1918 as one half of a coupled set of vehicles designed to convey produce from North Kent to markets in Central London. It is not known whether this wartime "freight train" was ever used, but the pair of trams certainly did figure as a makeshift staff transport during a rail strike in 1924. Car 014 ended its career separated from its twin and rebuilt as a railgrinder equipped with two water tanks. (R.Elliott)

91. All systems go for the changeover and some interested spectators have gathered at the depot to watch the final hours of the trams. The old entrance has been enlarged to accommodate the new fleet which is safely under cover to the left of the tower wagon. (C.Carter)

92. The tracks from the depot to Chingford have now been tarred over leaving only a single spur leading to the scrapyard round the back. (C.F.Klapper)

93. Car 1679 is frozen in time just before it bites the dust at the last round up of M class cars behind Walthamstow Depot. Car 1468 to the rear has already been desecrated by official vandals. Such was the melancholy fate of the vast London tram fleet. (D.W.K.Jones)

94. Chingford Road still presents a semi-rural aspect as a top covered car waits at a passing loop. The Walthamstow tramways were originally constructed with a minimum of double track; this soon proved to be a mistake as traffic grew. Note also the narrow spacing of the overhead wires, which were suspended at a height of 22ft. 6ins./6.8 metres above the road, and the two skates fixed to the overhead which activated signals controlling the single track sections. (R.J.Harley Coll.)

95. Car 16 halts to pick up passengers in Chingford Road. This tram had already been rebuilt by the council with a six window lower saloon instead of the original three window layout. (B.J.Cross Coll.)

96. Shadows fall across car 285 on the last day
of tram services to Chingford Mount. This
former West Ham car 97 is performing one of
the final duties on service 87. (L.A.Gibson)

LT circular issued in May 1935

641.—ALTERATIONS TO SERVICES.

Notice to Inspectors and Conductors—Bow, Leyton, Walthamstow and West Ham Depots.

    (i.) Extension of Service No. 87 to Chingford—Daily.

    (ii.) Withdrawal of Service No. 10 and Institution of Transfer facilities.

Commencing on Thursday, 4th April, 1935, Service No. 87 will be extended to Chingford Mount, daily. A farebill is exhibited in the depot and should be closely studied for through fares.

On the same date Service No. 10 (West Ham), will be withdrawn, and the following new transfer fares will be instituted :—

Fares.	Journey.	Change Point.	Services affected.
1d. Ordinary	Hamfrith Road—West Ham Church...	} Stratford Broadway	63; 1, 1a, 69, 97, 99.
1½d. Ordinary	" Princess Alice "—West Ham Church		
1½d. Ordinary	Hamfrith Road—Plaistow Station ...	Stratford Broadway	
2d. Workmen's Return & ∫	" Princess Alice "—Plaistow Station ...	Stratford Broadway	} 63 ; 69, 97, 99.
3d. Ordinary Return {	Hamfrith Road—Plaistow Broadway	Stratford Broadway	

Transfers at children's rates will not be provided but transfer tickets at adult fares will be issued to children on request.

The sections on the 1d. and 1½d. tickets for use on Services No. 1, 1a, 69, 73, 95, have been re-arranged and numbered.

The method of punching and cancelling transfer tickets is as follows :—

    On Issue.—Punch in appropriate transfer section above double line.

    Second Car (forward journey)—Cancel below double line on same edge as punch hole.

    Return Journey—Cancel above and below double line on uncancelled edge on first and second cars respectively. Specimens of revised tickets will be exhibited in the depots.

97. The Crooked Billet was an important "halfway" stop on the road to Chingford Mount. Here a tram is about to reverse for the journey back to Lea Bridge Road. In the centre of the picture is a traction standard bearing a FARE STAGE notice as well as the white letters CARS STOP HERE on a red background. (A.J.Watkins Coll.)

98. The arrival of the trams stimulated housing growth around Chingford Mount, thus also generating more passengers for the system. Here car 1, in original condition, poses at the end of the line opposite the Prince Albert public house. (B.J.Cross Coll.)

99. A quarter of a century on from the previous view and car 24 no longer has the road to itself. It must compete with a clutch of independent buses all intent on poaching as many passengers as they could away from the tramways. On a technical note, the detail of car 24's swivel head trolley can clearly be seen. (G.N.Southerden)

100. LCC car 1723 stands in front of a Walthamstow bogie car in this 1931 view. Both trams offered a greater standard of comfort than the old open top vehicles, and as such they were able to win back many of the customers who had deserted to motor bus competitors. (G.N.Southerden)

101. A final look at Chingford Mount terminus reveals LT car 566 operating one of the last journeys. It is already taking power from the new trolleybus overhead. On the right, the

Prince Albert is undergoing one of its periodic renovations. In more modern times this building was demolished to be replaced by a supermarket. (A.B.Cross)

ROLLING STOCK

The Walthamstow fleet started life in typically British fashion with a number of four wheel, open top cars. An increase in passengers and subsequent demands for better vehicles in bad weather resulted in a car rebuilding programme and the introduction of top covered upper decks. It is to the council's credit that they kept faith with the tramcar and were able to order newer, more powerful vehicles to match other tramway operators in joint services across East London and into the heart of the metropolis. The trams in the last batch of Walthamstow bogie cars have gone down in tramway folklore as some of the fastest vehicles on eight wheels ever to operate in the capital.

Walthamstow livery was crimson lake and chrome yellow, with the lettering -
WALTHAMSTOW DISTRICT COUNCIL in gold shaded red.

Cars 1-32. These were ordered from Brush of Loughborough for the opening of the system in 1905. They were of a conventional open top design and they rode on Brush 21E trucks of 6ft./1828mm wheelbase. All of these vehicles were later rebuilt with new lower saloon windows. Top covers were also added, although open balconies were retained. Many trams in this class were equipped with longer wheelbase trucks before the whole batch passed to London Transport in 1933.

Cars 33-38. These covered top, single truck cars were built by Hurst, Nelson in 1910. They used Hurst, Nelson 21E trucks of 8ft./2439mm wheelbase. These cars were later equipped with transverse seating.

Cars 39-46. These single deck, bogie cars were originally built at Preston in 1902. Their first owner was Oldham Corporation, but they later passed to Rotherham and were third hand when they arrived in East London. They ran on equal wheel, Brill 27G trucks. They were not repainted by London Transport and the whole batch was scrapped in 1934.

Cars 47-52. These were ex-London United type W cars which had been built by BEC in 1902 to run on Brill 22E trucks. These six trams were acquired by Walthamstow in 1920 and were repainted and renumbered. They had all been withdrawn and scrapped by 1932.

→

102. Just delivered and ready for service, car 3 shows all the elegance and craftmanship of the traditional four wheel, open top tram. (Walthamstow official photo)

Cars 53-64. This batch of twelve bogie cars was delivered from Hurst, Nelson in 1927. They had conduit equipment to work over LCC lines. After transfer to London Transport they received windscreens and they ended their days in the early 1950s working in South London.

Cars 39-46 (second series). Ordered in 1932, these vehicles were built by Brush and rode on maximum traction trucks from the same manufacturer. Plough carriers were included as standard and the whole batch was delivered already fitted with windscreens.

Water Car. This vehicle came with a 1,500 gallon water tank and was purchased from Brush in 1905. Sometime later it received a shed like body with a new trolley base; it was renumbered 63K by London Transport.

→

103. Extra revenue could be gathered by the display of local advertising on the cars. Here car 8 has been liberally adorned with trade messages; this tram also carries boards which denote it as the Rising Sun to Napier Arms shuttle car. (B.J.Cross Coll.)

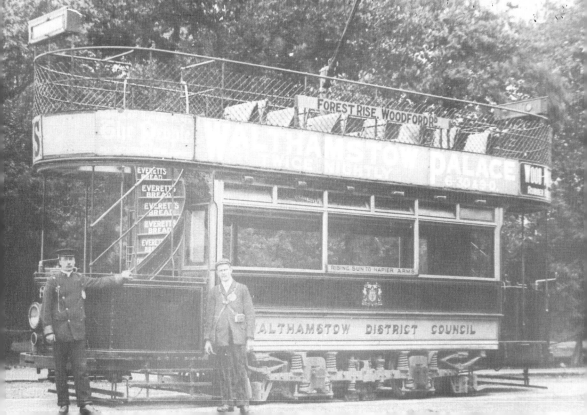

105. Car 25 retains its original 6ft. wheelbase truck, but has a rebuilt six window lower saloon. It also retains longitudinal bench seats on the lower deck. Note that the title of the undertaking has now lost its gold letters and has assumed the form of small black lettering on the rocker panel. This view dates from 1928. (H.Nicol)

104. An end view of car 22 gives all those details so beloved of tramway modellers. The fleet number was in gold shaded red and the trucks and undergear were painted black. (B.J.Cross Coll.)

106. Car 2 has been extensively rebuilt and has been fitted with transverse seats in the lower saloon. Additionally it has received an 8ft. wheelbase truck. The bogus coat of arms on the waist panel was substituted by new municipal arms when Walthamstow became a borough in 1929. (H.Nicol)

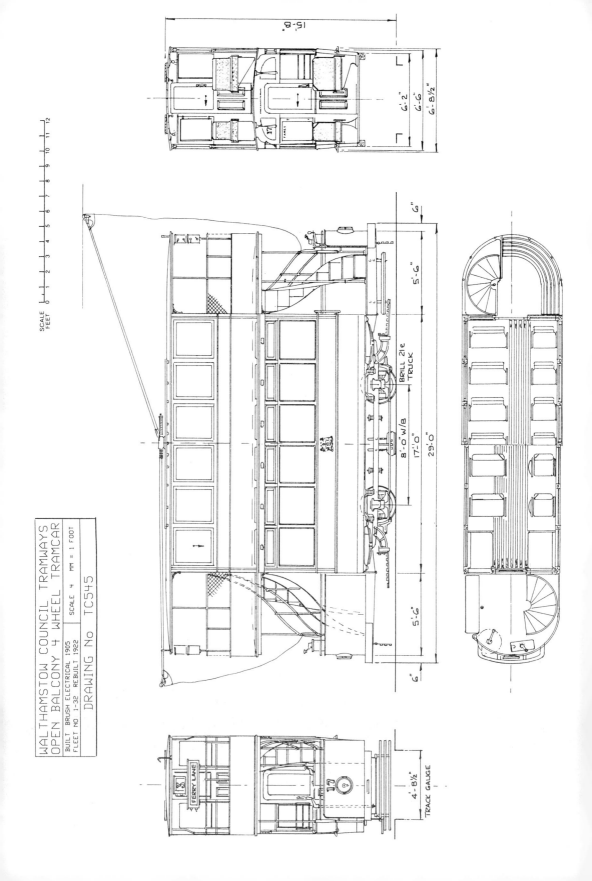

SCALE
FEET 0 1 2 3 4 5 6 7 8 9 10 11 12

WALTHAMSTOW COUNCIL TRAMWAYS
OPEN BALCONY 4 WHEEL TRAMCAR

BUILT BRUSH ELECTRICAL 1905   REBUILT 1922
FLEET No 1-32   SCALE 4   MM = 1 FOOT

DRAWING No TC545

15'-8"

6'-2"
6'-6"
6'-8½"

6"
5'-6"
BRILL 21e TRUCK
8'-0" w/B
17'-0"
29'-0"
5'-6"
6"

FERRY LANE

17

4'-8½"
TRACK GAUGE

107. LT car 2012 was formerly Walthamstow car 9, and it is pictured in London Transport red and cream livery with the attractive LCC style gold numerals. This tram also has double trolleys; it finally went for scrap in 1936/7. (G.N.Southerden)

108. This tram from the 33-38 series was acquired to work the joint services to Stratford and the Docks. Note the lower saloon curtains and the advertising transparencies along the tops of the lower windows. (B.J.Cross Coll.)

109. Ex-Walthamstow car 38, now LT car 2030, is seen in fair condition very shortly before its demise. (C.Carter)

110. The single deckers acquired in 1919 helped maintain the Higham Hill to Markhouse Road service. The vehicle depicted here is in splendid condition; each window is engraved with a patterned border and the passengers sit facing one another on bench seats. The car has a clerestory roof with top lights which could be opened for extra ventilation. (G.N.Southerden)

DRAWN BY:- TERRY RUSSELL, "CHACESIDE", ST. LEONARDS PARK, HORSHAM, W.SUSSEX. RH13 6EG.
SEND 3 FIRST CLASS STAMPS FOR COMPLETE LIST OF PUBLIC TRANSPORT DRAWINGS.

SCALE FEET 0 1 2 3 4 5 6 7 8 9 10

WALTHAMSTOW COUNCIL TRAMWAYS
SINGLE DECK 8W TRAMCAR

BUILT E R & T Co 1902 No 39-46 | SCALE 4 MM = 1 FOOT
EX ROTHERHAM & OLDHAM

DRAWING No TC546

MAIN SIDE WINDOWS WERE
ETCHED IN LINES AS SHOWN.

11'-2"

6'-5½"
6'-9"
7'-0"

6"
4'-0"

BRILL 27G
BOGIE

4'-0"

14'-6'
26'-0'
35'-0'

4'-0"

6"

4'-0"

4'-8½"
TRACK GAUGE

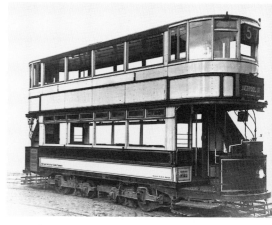

111. Car 52 originally formed part of the large LUT fleet and it spent its declining years shuttling between Higham Hill and Markhouse Road in company with the single deck cars. Note the split "Robinson" staircase on these cars and the lack of any covered protection for the motorman and conductor. Similar cars are featured in the Middleton Press album *Kingston and Wimbledon Tramways*. (G.N.Southerden)

112. The 1926 Hurst, Nelson cars were sturdy vehicles as this view testifies. The low dash partly conceals large BTH type 521B controllers; another feature was the placing of the fleet number next to the headlight, rather than above or below as was traditional. (Hurst, Nelson official photo)

113. The final additions to the fleet comprised these handsome eight wheel cars built by Brush. Each vehicle had seats for 27 in the lower saloon and 42 in the upper saloon.

Unlike the previous Hurst, Nelson cars, this series came equipped with body mounted plough carriers. (R.Elliott)

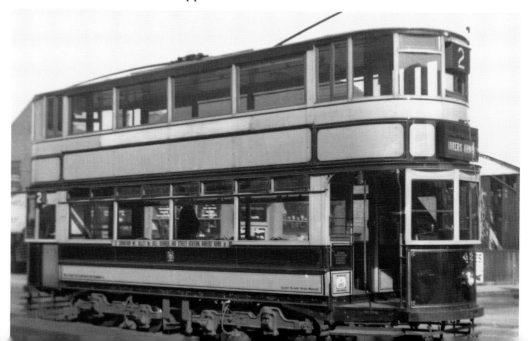

SCALE
FEET | 0 1 2 3 4 5 6 7 8 9 10

DRAWN BY FRANK KOCHE AND KINDLY MADE AVAILABLE THROUGH:
--TERRY RUSSELL, "CHACESIDE", ST.LEONARDS PARK, HORSHAM, W.SUSSEX. RH13 6EG.
SEND 3 FIRST CLASS STAMPS FOR COMPLETE LIST OF PUBLIC TRANSPORT DRAWINGS.

OVER GUARD RAILS

7'2"

6'10"

2'1"

FARE
BILL

YELLOW
LINE

2'-3¾"

WHITBREAD'S ALE & STOUT

LONDON TRANSPORT

13

2'-0"
4'-6"
4'-6"
1'-10"
2'-0"
22'-2" BODY
33'-10" OVER FENDERS.

13

ALDERSGATE

4'-8½"

BLACK
CREAM
BLACK
RED
BLACK
CREAM
BLACK
RED
BLACK
GREY

| WALTHAMSTOW COUNCIL TRAMWAYS |
| TOTALLY ENCLOSED 8W TRAMCAR |

BUILT HURST NELSON 1926	SCALE 4 MM = 1 FOOT
FLEET No 53-64 TYPE LCC E1	
DRAWING No TC547	

UPPER SALOON

LOWER SALOON

MOTOR HATCH

PLOUGH HATCH

MOTOR HATCH

DOOR

5'-4½"
2'0"
32'-4"
1'-3" 1'-3"
6' 6' 6'
6' 6' 6'
1'-10⅞"
2'-0"

7'2"

6'-8"

114. Car 2058 is at Enfield terminus on service 29 in pre-war days. This tram, which was formerly Walthamstow car 43, presents an interesting contrast in styles with the Feltham type car in front. (G.N.Southerden)

115. We look along the shapely, arch-backed seats of the lower saloon towards the motorman's platform. The bulkhead door is open to reveal the large BTH controller. (D.Jones Coll.)

116. This substantial looking machine would lay the dust and the revolving brush at the back would sweep the tracks clear. Snow clearance by means of the inclined plates was another one of its functions. (R.I.Close)

117. Pictured in its last guise before disposal, the water car has at least acquired some rudementary shelter for the crew. Underneath the cream painted body is a Brush AA, 6ft. wheelbase truck. (D.W.K.Jones)

FINALE

118. The camera records a poignant moment at Grove Park as the crew stand either side of car 2043. This rather battered ex-Walthamstow vehicle does the honours as the last ever service 52 tram on 5th January 1952. (D.Jones Coll.)

119. Areas which were once served by Walthamstow and Leyton trams could still be traversed by trolleybus until this form of transport was also banished from the local streets in April 1960. Here a trolleybus on route 581 nears Whipps Cross; disused tramtracks are still in the roadway. (C.Carter)

120. The Walthamstow tram trundles into history. We are left to wonder whether, in contrast to today's fume filled congestion, we shall ever again experience the simple delights of an unhurried tram ride to Epping Forest. (G.N.Southerden)

MP Middleton Press

Easebourne Lane, Midhurst, West Sussex. GU29 9AZ
Tel: 01730 813169   Fax: 01730 812601

Write or telephone for our detailed catalogue of
transport, military and local history albums, books and videos

Tramway Classics

Bournemouth & Poole Tramways

Bristol's Tramways

Brighton's Tramways

Camberwell & West Norwood Tramways

Croydon's Tramways

Dover's Tramways

East Ham & West Ham Tramways

Embankment & Waterloo Tramways

Exeter & Taunton Tramways

Greenwich & Dartford Tramways

Hampstead & Highgate Tramways

Hastings Tramways

Ilford and Barking Tramways

Kingston & Wimbledon Tramways

Lewisham & Catford Tramways

Maidstone & Chatham Tramways

North Kent Tramways

Southend-on-Sea Tramways

Southampton's Tramways

Southwark & Deptford Tramways

Thanet's Tramways

Victoria & Lambeth Tramways

Wandsworth & Battersea Tramways

London Railway Albums

Clapham Junction to Beckenham Junction

Charing Cross to Orpington

Crystal Palace (High Level) and Catford Loop

Holborn Viaduct to Lewisham

London Bridge to Addiscombe

London Bridge to East Croydon

Mitcham Junction Lines

South London Line

Victoria to Bromley South

West Croydon to Epsom

Waterloo to Windsor

96